NBA CHAMPIONSHIPS:

↓

NONE

↓

ALL-TIME LEADING SCORER:

↓

RANDY SMITH (1971–79, 1982–83):

↓

12,735 POINTS

THE NBA: A HISTORY OF HOOPS

LOS ANGELES CLIPPERS

BY JIM WHITING

CREATIVE EDUCATION CREATIVE PAPERBACKS

Published by Creative Education
and Creative Paperbacks

P.O. Box 227, Mankato, Minnesota 56002

Creative Education and Creative Paperbacks
are imprints of The Creative Company

www.thecreativecompany.us

Design and production by Blue Design

Printed in the United States of America

Photographs by AP Images (ASSOCIATED PRESS),
Larry Berman, Corbis (Bettmann), Getty Images
(Andrew D. Bernstein/NBAE, Kevork Djansezian/
Getty Images Sport, Stephen Dunn/Allsport,
Garrett W. Ellwood/NBAE, Focus on Sport/
Getty Images Sport, Sean Gardner/Getty Images
Sport, George Gojkovich, Noah Graham/NBAE,
Tim Heitman/NBAE, David Hofmann, Andy
Lyons/Getty Images Sport, John W. McDonough/
Sports Illustrated, Peter Read Miller/Sports
Illustrated, Mike Powell/NBAE, Dick Raphael/
NBAE, Rick Stewart/NBAE), Newscom (JOHN
ANGELILLO/UPI, FREDERIC J. BROWN/AFP/
Getty Images, TANNEN MAURY/EPA, JON
SOOHOO/EPA, Harry E. Walker/MCT)

Library of Congress Cataloging-in-Publication Data

Names: Whiting, Jim, 1943- author.

Title: Los Angeles Clippers / Jim Whiting.

Series: The NBA: A History of Hoops.

Includes bibliographical references and index.

Summary: This high-interest title summarizes the
history of the Los Angeles Clippers professional
basketball team, highlighting memorable events
and noteworthy players such as Chris Paul.

Identifiers: LCCN 2016054012 / ISBN 978-1-60818-
847-5 (hardcover) / ISBN 978-1-62832-450-1
(pbk) / ISBN 978-1-56660-895-4 (eBook)

Subjects: LCSH: 1. Los Angeles Clippers
(Basketball team)—History—Juvenile
literature. 2. Los Angeles Clippers (Basketball
team)—Biography—Juvenile literature.

Classification: LCC GV885.52.L65 W544 2017 /
DDC 796.323/640979494—dc23

CCSS: RI.4.1, 2, 3, 4; RI.5.1, 2, 4; RI.6.1, 2,
3; RF.4.3, 4; RF.5.3, 4; RH. 6-8. 4, 5, 7

First Edition HC 9 8 7 6 5 4 3 2 1

First Edition PBK 9 8 7 6 5 4 3 2 1

CONTENTS

8

One of the world's most famous
cities, **LOS ANGELES** is home
to two pro basketball teams.

BIRTH OF THE BRAVES

Generally a team's highlights consist of highflying dunks, incredible come-from-behind wins, and raising championship banners. One of the greatest highlights for the Los Angeles Clippers

10

happened far from a basketball court. On December 14, 2011, the National Basketball Association (NBA) approved a big trade. Superstar point guard Chris Paul would go from the New Orleans Hornets to the Clippers. The Clippers had just 6 winning seasons in their 40-year history. Many called them the "Paper Clips" because they were so bad. Paul came at a high cost. The Clippers had to give up four outstanding players. "We decided for a player of Chris's caliber that it was just time to make the move and push all our chips into the center of the table," said Clippers vice president of basketball operations Neil Olshey. "He's a warrior, and he's going to take this whole organization to the next level." Would Paul live up to those lofty expectations? Or would the Clippers continue losing?

The Clippers' story began in 1970 on the opposite side of the country. The NBA was enjoying increasing popularity. The league

All-Star **CHRIS PAUL** led the league in steals per game in three Clippers seasons.

GOOOOOOOALLLLLL!

RANDY SMITH, GUARD/SMALL FORWARD, 6-FOOT-3, 1971–79, 1982–83

Randy Smith was a soccer All-American in college. He also led his the basketball team to three straight league championships. "If all things had been equal, I probably would have chosen soccer," Smith said in 1976. "That's what I was gearing for, but the average salary of a soccer player is $10,000. The average NBA salary is $105,000. I didn't have a choice." Soccer was still in his blood. He tried out with the Tampa Bay Rowdies of the North American Soccer League in 1975. The team offered him a contract. The Braves wouldn't let him play. He tried twice more. He was cut. He'd been away from soccer too long.

decided to expand. It granted franchises to Portland, Oregon; Cleveland, Ohio; and Buffalo, New York. Each team's first task was selecting a name. In Buffalo, more than 14,000 fans submitted suggestions. The most popular entry was Frontiersmen. Seventy-four people suggested it. Team officials chose Braves instead. They wanted to honor the region's American Indian heritage. "We wanted a name that not only symbolized what the athlete would do on the court but one that would also be representative of the city of Buffalo," said team president Carl Scheer.

Buffalo officials assembled the team. The Braves received several players from other teams. They also participated in the 1970 NBA Draft. Many fans wanted them to select Calvin Murphy. He was a 5-foot-9 guard from nearby Niagara University. He had averaged 33 points a game in college. Instead, Buffalo chose forward John Hummer of

After a stellar rookie season, guard **ERNIE DiGREGORIO** suffered from knee injuries.

Princeton University. Murphy went on to a Hall-of-Fame career. Hummer averaged fewer than nine points per game in three seasons. Then Buffalo traded him. This was the first of many confusing personnel moves. The Braves struggled to a 22–60 mark that first season. They posted similar marks the following two years.

Fortunately, their draft choices improved. They took Randy Smith in 1971. Though he was a seventh-round choice, Smith was a gifted athlete. He high-jumped 6 feet, 10 inches in college. At training camp, coach Dolph Schayes watched Smith easily outpace his teammates during a series of drills. "He's fast," Schayes said. "He's staying." In 1972, the Braves chose power forward/center Bob McAdoo. He was named Rookie of the Year. "I used to think he took bad shots, but I've changed my mind," said Milwaukee Bucks center Kareem Abdul-Jabbar. "Nobody takes shots from where McAdoo does and hits like he does." Buffalo added guard Ernie DiGregorio in the 1973 NBA Draft. He also became Rookie of the Year. These additions helped Buffalo make the playoffs that season. They lost in the first round. The same thing happened in 1974–75. The Braves went 46–36 the following season. They won their first-ever playoff series. But they lost in the second round.

16

TRANS-CONTINENTAL TREK

he wheels started coming off in the 1976–77 season. Buffalo traded McAdoo. They obtained future Hall-of-Famer Moses Malone only to trade him

With 34.5 points per game, scoring leader **BOB McADOO** was league MVP in 1974–75.

IN A LEAGUE BY HIMSELF

BILL WALTON, CENTER, 6-FOOT-11, 1979–85

Bill Walton grew up in La Mesa. It is a few miles east of San Diego. He led UCLA to two national championships. He was College Player of the Year three times. He was named NBA Finals MVP in 1977 when Portland won the championship. He became the league's MVP the following season. After leaving the Clippers, he played for the Boston Celtics. He received the NBA Sixth Man Award in 1986. He is the only player to win all three NBA awards. In 1996, Walton was named among of the 50 greatest players in NBA history.

LEGENDS OF THE HARDWOOD

after just two games. Forward Adrian Dantley became the third Braves player in five years to be named Rookie of the Year. He was traded at the end of the season. The team plunged to 30 wins. It managed just 27 in 1977–78. One of the few highlights that season came when Smith scored 27 points in the All-Star Game. He was named the game's Most Valuable Player (MVP). "Being a seventh-round draft choice, it was a brilliant opportunity to show everyone that I belonged in the NBA," he said.

The Braves' dismal record kept fans away. That set the stage for an unusual change of ownership. Movie producer Irv Levin had purchased the Boston Celtics in 1972. He lived in California. He wanted to move the team there. But the NBA would never allow that. Boston was the most successful and iconic team in the NBA. Few teams in professional sports were so closely identified with their cities. So Levin approached Buffalo owner John Y. Brown. He offered to swap franchises with him. Brown was a shrewd businessman. He had made his fortune by buying Kentucky Fried Chicken from Col. Harlan Sanders and selling thousands of KFC franchises. He knew the Celtics were much more popular than the Braves. He agreed to the deal.

Brown now owned the Celtics. Levin was the new owner of the Braves. Levin might have been able to include Celtics forward Larry Bird in the deal. He decided not to. Of course, Bird enjoyed one of the greatest careers in NBA history—for the Celtics. Levin moved the Braves to San

19

Known as the "Prince of Midair," **WORLD B. FREE** could sink shots from anywhere.

Diego. That city's NBA team, the Rockets, had moved to Houston in 1970. Levin renamed his new team the Clippers. Clippers were graceful sailing ships. They sailed across the Pacific Ocean from San Diego and nearby ports during the nineteenth century.

The "Clips," as people began calling them, became somewhat graceful in their new home. They were led by guard Lloyd Free. Soon, he changed his name to World B. Free. In 1978–79, he averaged nearly 29 points a game, taking shots from seemingly impossible angles. "People come right out of their seats when I do my thing," Free boasted. "People want to see that razzle-dazzle. They like seeing guys taking crazy shots and hitting them." San Diego sailed to a 43–39 record. It wasn't good enough to make the playoffs. Smith was traded after the season. The next year, Free averaged 30 points a game. But the Clippers traded him, too.

LEGENDS OF THE HARDWOOD

DRAFT-DAY DISASTERS

In the 1982 NBA Draft, the Clippers chose power forward Terry Cummings. He became Rookie of the Year. In 2003, the Clippers chose center Chris Kaman (pictured). He became an All-Star. In the 21 years in between, the Clippers had only one top draft pick who became a solid performer for them. That was power forward Danny Manning in 1988. The others were busts. A few did play well—after the Clippers traded them. During those two decades of poor draft choices, the Clippers had a single winning season. No other NBA team has had such a dismal streak.

22

OUT TO DRY

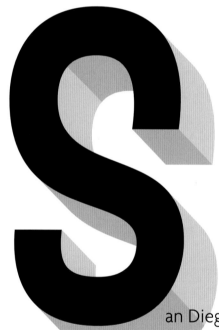an Diego took a gamble in 1979. The Clippers traded several key players for local favorite Bill Walton. He had led the Portland Trail Blazers to the 1977 NBA championship. With the Clippers, he struggled with a series of injuries. Walton missed two entire seasons. In 1981, Donald Sterling

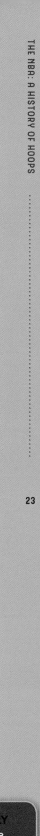

Bruising forward **TERRY CUMMINGS** gave the Clippers instant scoring power.

Steady-scoring swingman **MARQUES JOHNSON** couldn't lift the team to the postseason.

bought the team. He was a Los Angeles attorney and businessman. San Diego won just 17 games that season. It was the team's worst-ever record. Rookie forward Tom Chambers was one of the few bright spots. He led the team with 17 points a game. The team selected Terry Cummings in the 1982 NBA Draft. He was named Rookie of the Year. Both players were gone by the end of the 1983–84 season. So was Randy Smith. He had returned to the team for 1982–83. During that season, he set an iron-man record. Starting in 1972, he had played in 906 games in a row. Once again, though, a strong player was traded away.

Sterling publicly said he would keep the Clippers in San Diego. But he really wanted to move them to Los Angeles, where he lived. The NBA already had a successful franchise in Los Angeles, the Lakers. Sterling moved them anyway. He didn't ask the league's permission. The NBA fined him $6 million. Walton played one season

Top overall draft pick **DANNY MANNING** was a two-time All-Star in Los Angeles.

with the Clippers in Los Angeles. Then he was traded to Boston. He shouldered the blame for the team's poor showing and its move. "I'm personally responsible for the failure of the Clippers in San Diego," he later said.

In their new home, the Clippers won only 31 games the first season. Rookie power forward Michael Cage became an instant fan favorite for his ferocious rebounding. The Clippers won 32 games in the second season. Then they plummeted to 17 wins in 1987–88. The team chose Danny Manning in the 1988 NBA Draft. He had been College Player of the Year. It didn't help. He was hurt most of the year. The Clippers went 21–61. After two more losing seasons, the Clippers finally found success in 1991–92. They won 45 games and slipped into the playoffs for the first time in 15 years. It was the longest postseason drought in NBA history. But they lost in the first round to the Utah Jazz, three games to two. A

LEGENDS OF THE HARDWOOD

TAKING THE TITLE

MICHAEL CAGE, POWER FORWARD, 6-FOOT-9, 1984–88

Michael Cage was nicknamed "Windexman." The name refers to the famous window-cleaning product. His rebounding ability was often referred to as "cleaning the glass." In the last game of the 1987–88 season, Cage needed 28 rebounds to win the league rebounding title. "At the end of the third quarter, I had 19 rebounds," Cage said, "but I was exhausted. I had nothing left in the tank." Somehow he pulled down 11 more rebounds in the final quarter. He finished with 30. It was his last game as a Clipper. He became yet another great player the Clippers traded away.

Forward **LAMAR ODOM** displayed effortless speed and ball-handling ability.

41–41 record the following year was good enough for another playoffs appearance. But the Houston Rockets sank them in the first round.

The Clippers returned to their losing ways the following season ... and the one after that ... and so on. The Clippers hit bottom in 1998–99. They scraped together only nine wins. They attracted the fewest fans in the league. In 1999, the Clippers moved into the Staples Center. The arena was also the Lakers' home. The two teams went in opposite directions. The Lakers won the NBA championship. The Clippers finished with a league-worst 15–67 mark. In 2001, though, the Clippers added some much-needed star power. They traded for Elton Brand. He was a powerful young forward. "Brand gives us more rebounding," said Clippers general manager Elgin Baylor. "He's a good shot blocker and can run the floor also." It didn't matter. The Clippers continued losing.

High-scoring forward **ELTON BRAND** led the Clippers to the playoffs in 2006.

SETTING SAIL

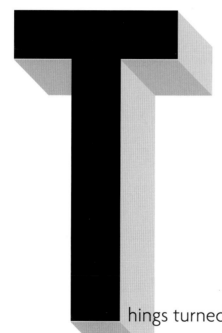

hings turned around in 2004–05. The
Clippers had a better record (37–45) than the Lakers
(34–48). They built on that momentum the following
season. Their 47–35 mark was the first winning season in
13 years. The Clippers won their first playoff series in 30
years. They beat the Denver Nuggets four games to one.

As a rookie, guard **ERIC GORDON** notched 41 points in a single game.

32

They nearly topped the Phoenix Suns in the second round before losing four games to three.

The Clippers slid backward for the next five years. The low point came in 2008–09. Los Angeles won just 19 games. But the team was quietly setting a course for better days. In 2008, the team drafted center DeAndre Jordan. He recorded 10 dunks in a single game. Only two other rookies had ever done that. The Clips drafted power forward Blake Griffin the following year. He suffered a preseason knee injury and missed the entire regular season. In 2010–11, Griffin was named Rookie of the Year and played in the All-Star Game. *Sports Illustrated* named him one of the 15 greatest rookies of all time. "I think it's been a while since there's been a rookie as good as him," teammate Chris Kaman said. "LeBron [James], Carmelo [Anthony] maybe. But it's not the same. They didn't do for their teams what he does for our team."

During their first 46 years, the Clippers made the playoffs just 12 times.

WORST. OWNER. EVER?

In 2000, *Sports Illustrated* ran a story about the Clippers. It was titled "The Worst Franchise in Sports History." The story blamed owner Donald Sterling for the team's misfortunes. "I'll build the Clippers through the draft, free agency, trades, spending whatever it takes to make a winner," Sterling said when he bought the team. None of that was true. He delayed paying his players. He asked coach Paul Silas to serve as team trainer. Every other team had a separate trainer. Nothing changed when the team moved to Los Angeles. In 2014, recordings of Sterling making racist comments became public. The NBA made him sell the team.

In 2011, **BLAKE GRIFFIN** was the first rookie chosen for the All-Star Game since 2003.

The two highfliers had ignited a spark. That spark burst into flames in the 2011–12 season. The Clippers reversed years of bad player decisions. They signed superstar point guard Chris Paul. He became the first Clippers player named to the All-NBA First Team. Griffin made the Second Team. Los Angeles surged to 40–26 in the strike-shortened season. Its winning percentage of .606 was the best in team history. The Clippers defeated the Memphis Grizzlies in the opening round of the playoffs. It was just their third-ever playoff series win. Then the Spurs swept them in the second round.

A NEW STAR SHINES

That season was just the start. Fans enjoyed watching Paul's high looping passes to Jordan, Griffin, and other teammates. They began to refer to the team as "Lob City." ESPN sportswriter Arash Markazi

A dunking machine, **GRIFFIN** brought fans back to fill up the Staples Center.

40

HONORING HIS GRANDFATHER

CHRIS PAUL, POINT GUARD, 6 FEET, 2011–PRESENT

Chris Paul's grandfather, Nathaniel Jones, owned a service station. He closed early for Paul's high school games. In 2002, Jones was beaten to death. He was 61. Paul's aunt suggested he try to score 61 points in his next game. Paul didn't think he could. But he hit 61 with less than two minutes left. Then he was fouled. "I walked to the free throw line, [the referee] gave me the ball and I shot an air ball right out of bounds," Paul said. He left the game and started crying. If he had stayed in, Paul might have set a state record for points in a game. That didn't matter. He'd honored his grandfather.

LEGENDS OF THE HARDWOOD

said, "Like most good nicknames, it eventually took on a life of its own, and the Clippers are living up to it on a nightly basis, with lob dunks so spectacular they instantly become trending topics on Twitter." The Clippers had a 25–6 mark at the end of December in the 2012–13 season, the best in the NBA. It included a team-best 17-game winning streak. They finished 56–26, their best record in history. They swept the Lakers during the regular season for the first time since 1974–75. They also won the Western Conference's Pacific Division for the first time. The Clippers took a 2–0 lead over the Memphis Grizzlies in the first round of the playoffs. Unfortunately, Griffin sprained his ankle during practice and was sidelined. The Grizzlies won the next four games.

Griffin returned to form in 2013–14. The Clippers added seasoned veterans such as shooting guards J. J. Redick and Jamal

42

JAMAL CRAWFORD received the NBA's Sixth Man of the Year award in 2015–16.

Crawford. Lob City sailed to 57 wins. Again they were Pacific Division champions. They defeated the Golden State Warriors in the first round of the playoffs, four games to three. They couldn't get past Oklahoma City in the next round, though. The Clippers went 56–26 in the following season. They defeated San Antonio in the first round of the playoffs. The Clippers took a 3–1 lead over Houston in the next round. But the Rockets won three games in a row to take the series. "The Clipper curse when I first got here was No. 1 picks getting hurt, not working out, their

Defensive-minded forward **GLEN DAVIS** brought energy to Los Angeles.

J. J. REDICK boosted the Clippers to the playoffs again in 2016.

> "THE CLIPPER CURSE WHEN I FIRST GOT HERE WAS NO. 1 PICKS GETTING HURT, NOT WORKING OUT, THEIR DRAFT PICKS NOT WORKING OUT, NOT MAKING THE PLAYOFFS, NOT HAVING WINNING SEASONS," GRIFFIN SAID.

draft picks not working out, not making the playoffs, not having winning seasons," Griffin said. "No one talked about not getting past the second round. Not a single soul talked about that. But now that's what everyone talks about. Just like the last one, we're going to bust through this one." The Clippers returned to the playoffs in 2015–16. Unfortunately, Griffin and Paul were both injured. The Trail Blazers bounced them out in the first round. That "bust through" would have to wait. The waiting continued in 2016–17. In a closely fought seven-game playoff series in which no game was decided by more than eight points, the resurgent Utah Jazz ended the Clippers' season. Losing Griffin to an injury during Game 3 was a major factor, as Utah won three of the last four games.

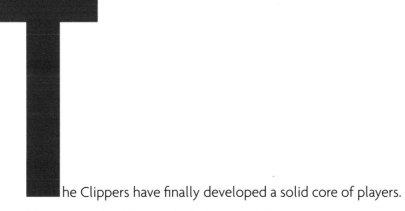

The Clippers have finally developed a solid core of players. The era of the "Paper Clips" has ended. The team's fans hope to soon "clip" an NBA championship banner to the rafters of the Staples Center.

THE NBA: A HISTORY OF HOOPS   LOS ANGELES CLIPPERS

SELECTED BIBLIOGRAPHY

Ballard, Chris. *The Art of a Beautiful Game: The Thinking Fan's Tour of the NBA*. New York: Simon & Schuster, 2010.

Hareas, John. *Ultimate Basketball: More Than 100 Years of the Sport's Evolution*. New York: DK, 2004.

Hubbard, Jan, ed. *The Official NBA Basketball Encyclopedia*. 3rd edition. New York: Doubleday, 2000.

NBA.com. "Los Angeles Clippers." http://www.nba.com/clippers/.

Simmons, Bill. *The Book of Basketball: The NBA According to the Sports Guy*. New York: Ballantine, 2009.

Sports Illustrated. *Sports Illustrated Basketball's Greatest*. New York: Sports Illustrated, 2014.

46

WEBSITES

DUCKSTERS BASKETBALL: NBA
http://www.ducksters.com/sports/national_basketball_association.php

Learn more about NBA history, rules, positions, strategy, drills, and other topics.

JR. NBA
http://jr.nba.com/

This kids site has games, videos, game results, team and player information, statistics, and more.

Note: Every effort has been made to ensure that any websites listed above were active at the time of publication. However, because of the nature of the Internet, it is impossible to guarantee that these sites will remain active indefinitely or that their contents will not be altered.

INDEX